A W

C000052319

Wordsworth Editions

First published in England 1993 by
Wordsworth Editions Ltd
Cumberland House
Crib Street
Ware
Hertfordshire SG12 9ET

ISBN 1 85326 991 3

Many illustrations in this
volume appear by courtesy
of the various breed societies

Set in $8\frac{1}{2}$/9pt Monophoto Univers Light
Text conversion and pagination by
August Filmsetting, St Helens

Printed in Italy by Amadeus s.p.a

Contents

Introduction 6
Hunting/gun: Pointer 10
German short-haired pointer 12
Golden retriever 14
Labrador retriever 16
English setter 18
Gordon setter 20
Irish setter 22
Cocker spaniel 24
English cocker spaniel 26
English springer spaniel 28
Field spaniel 30
Irish water spaniel 32
Sussex spaniel 34
Welsh springer spaniel 36
Working: Belgian sheepdog (Groenendael) 38
Border collie 40
Boxer 42
Bull mastiff 44
Rough collie 46
Dobermann Pinscher 48
German shepherd dog (Alsatian) 50
Great Dane 52
Mastiff 54
Old English sheepdog 56
Pyrenean mountain dog 58
Rottweiler 60
St Bernard 62
Samoyed 64

Siberian husky	66
Welsh corgi	68
Terriers: Airedale terrier	70
Australian terrier	72
Border terrier	74
Bull terrier	76
Cairn terrier	78
Dandie Dinmont	80
Fox terrier (wire-haired)	82
Irish terrier	84
Jack Russell terrier	86
Lakeland terrier	88
Norfolk terrier	90
Norwich terrier	92
Scottish terrier	94
Sealyham terrier	96
Skye terrier	98
Staffordshire bull terrier	100
Welsh terrier	102
West Highland White terrier	104
Toys: Cavalier King Charles spaniel	106
Chihuahua (smooth coat)	108
English Toy terrier (Black and Tan)	110
Griffin Bruxellois	112
Italian greyhound	114
Japanese Chin	116
King Charles spaniel	118
Löwchen	120
Maltese	122
Papillon	124
Pekingese	126

Pomeranian	128
Poodle (toy)	130
Pug	132
Yorkshire terrier	134
Utility: Boston terrier	136
Bulldog	138
Chow Chow	140
Dalmatian	142
French bulldog	144
Poodle (standard)	146
Schnauzer (standard)	148
Shih Tzû	150
Hounds: Afghan hound	152
Basenji	154
Basset hound	156
Beagle	158
Bloodhound	160
Borzoi	162
Dachshund (long-haired)	164
Dachshund (miniature smooth-haired)	166
Finnish Spitz	168
Greyhound	170
Irish Wolfhound	172
Otterhound	174
Pharoah hound	176
Rhodesian ridgeback	178
Saluki	180
Whippet	182
Glossary	184
Index	190

Introduction

Archaeological findings have identified the dog's distant ancestors on earth about 25 million years ago. Known as *Cynodesmus*, these evolved into *Tomarctus*, the direct ancestor of the wolf, which appeared in most parts of the world about 12,000 years ago. It was the first 'dog' to be domesticated by man, forming the longest-established friendship of man and animal.

Just how the wolf was domesticated is open to conjecture, but it is quite feasible that the wolf accepted scraps from the human settlements. As a good source of free food is never to be dismissed lightly, the wolf became more and more fearless and the humans more generous and welcoming, leading eventually to domestication.

Today's tame dog still has the same characteristics and behavioural patterns as its wild cousins, and even man's selection processes in developing specialist breeds have not altered such basic similarities as tail wagging, growling and the male's use of scent to mark out territory.

Different breeds developed naturally, depending on climate and environment, but it was the crossings, organised by man, that perfected the specialist breeds for working and hunting in its many forms, shepherding and guarding; thus giving rise to todays's classifications, including that of the straightforward companion.

The Arabs were the first to define the breeds, just as they had with the horse, and it is the Saluki that is regarded as being the first distinct recognised breed.

Man first employed the dog for hunting; by Roman times, dogs were also used to guard property, but following the fall of the Roman Empire the dog would seem to have disappeared until it re-emerged in medieval times, once more primarily for the task of hunting.

Real specialisation began in the Middle Ages, large guard dogs like the St Bernard and German shepherd being developed by monks. Pointers and setters were developed for hunting and terriers to go to ground. From here the racing dog and the companion were developed; demand grew and exchanges, sales and inter-breeding flourished throughout Europe.

In 1859, at Newcastle-upon-Tyne in England, the first dog show was held, limited to only hunting dogs. There were no set standards at that time, but there were about 50 entrants, enough to encourage the establishment of the English Kennel Club. This was founded in 1873, followed by the American Kennel Club in 1884 and the Italian Kennel Club in 1898. Today, the canine population is over 150 million.

The dog's highly-developed sense of smell is very important. Because it is at least 40 times greater than man's sense of smell, the dog is able to distinguish between odours that we are completely unaware of; between different meats and between different human beings – even twins – and can follow the tracks of animals even after some considerable time.

The dog's hearing is likewise highly developed, able to pick up ultrasonic vibrations that the human ear cannot, and also dogs are able to hear at far greater distances than us.

The dog's sense of taste proves more mysterious. Although it is closely related to the sense of smell, the dog will completely disregard taste if the food smells acceptable; if a small morsel of food is offered to the dog, it will first smell it before taking it in its mouth and then swallowing it without chewing.

Vision for dogs is definitely limited to black and white, but varies with the breed, and although breeders have generally improved dogs' sight, it still ranges between being able to distinguish shadowy movements to the sharp sight of the greyhound, which hunts by sight. The dog can see better at night than man, and the sheepdog's field of vision covers a 180° arc.

For each breed there is now an established standard which details the character of the dog, and this is upheld through the dog shows and Kennel Clubs around the world to ensure the continuation of the breed. In addition, is essential that the owners ensure the good health of the dog; although basically a healthy animal, it does need a good diet and sufficient exercise, the amount in each case varying with the breed. The dog must also be vaccinated against distemper, leptospirosis and infectious hepatitis, and be wormed regularly as a precaution.

The length of life of an individual dog depends on a number of factors, especially its breed. Some may live up to 20 years, others having a life-span of only 12 years. This chart relates the dog's age to ours.

Dog's age	Multiplier	Human age
2 months	7	14 months
6 months	10	5 years
8	12.5	9 years
12 months	14	14 years
18 months	13.3	20 years
2 years	12	24 years
3 years	10	30 years
4 years	9	36 years
5 years	8	40 years
6 years	7	42 years
7 years	7	49 years
8 years	7	56 years
9 years	7	63 years
10 years	6.5	65 years
11 years	6.5	71 years
12 years	6.3	75 years
13 years	6.2	80 years
14 years	6	84 years
15 years	5.8	87 years
16 years	5.6	89 years

Pointer

Description: an athletic dog, strong and agile; the name describes its motionless stance when pointing out the game with its nose

Head: the muzzle is slightly concave, with the nose raised

Eyes: hazel or chestnut, varying with coat colour

Ears: lie flat to the head, and are of medium length

Tail: long and tapering, and lashes from side to side in movement

Body: muscular thighs, front legs straight

Coat: smooth and shiny, with no feathering

Colour: lemon and white; orange and white; liver and white; black and white; self-colours and tricolours also allowed

Sizes: dogs' height 55.9cm (22-27in), bitches' height 53.3-66cm (21-26in); weight 20-30kg (44-66lb)

Origin: an outstanding dog, the result of much crossbreeding; it became established at the beginning of this century

Personality: a clever and affectionate dog, tolerant of children and obedient, with a good sense of smell

German short-haired pointer

Description: an elegant, distinguished-looking dog; also a powerful and speedy all-purpose gun dog

Head: clean cut; lean and well-delineated; neither too light nor too heavy, having a broad skull with a flat arch; prominent brown nose and a strong bite

Eyes: brown

Ears: flat with rounded points, set high

Tail: docked, so as to avoid self-injury during the hunt

Body: high-chested with well-arched ribs and moderately long neck; a short back

Coat: short, thick and coarse to the touch

Colour: liver; liver and white spotted to chest and limbs; liver and white spotted and ticked; liver and white ticked; as above, but with black replacing liver colouration

Sizes: dogs' height 58.4-63.5cm (23-25in), bitches height 53.3-58.4cm (21-23in); weight 25-32kg (55-70lb)

Origin: descended from the Spanish pointer, and introduced to Germany in the early seventeenth century by the Flemish. Crossbreeding has improved its speed and strength.

Personality: intelligent and decisive; excellent in the field and friendly with children

Golden retriever

Description: solid, robust dogs with a kindly charm

Head: a large, powerful muzzle with a strong bite; a clear frontal stop

Eyes: dark

Ears: of medium size

Tail: long, not curled

Body: well-balanced with an ample chest and muscular neck; muscular thighs and well-boned legs

Coat: shining and wavy, with a water-resistant undercoat and good feathering

Colour: gold or cream in any shading; red shades are not acceptable

Sizes: dogs' height 55.9-61cm (22-24in), bitches' height 50.8-57.1cm (20-22.5in); dogs' weight 29.5-34.1kg (65-75lb), bitches' weight 27.3-31.8kg (60-70lb)

Origin: the origin of the golden retriever is unclear, but it was certainly the result of a cross-breed some time in the mid-nineteenth century

Personality: one of the most popular of breeds; they make excellent companions, being patient and gentle with children

Labrador retriever

Description: a short, solid dog; an excellent retriever, working well in water or marshland
Head: pointed head with thick nose, strong bite and pronounced stop
Eyes: chestnut or hazel
Ears: hanging against the head
Tail: of medium length, very thick at the base and gradually tapering towards the tip; covered in special short thick hair, giving a rounded appearance
Body: well-boned legs, and a powerful neck
Coat: water resistant, short, dense and without waves
Colour: black or yellow but other colours allowed
Sizes: dogs' height 55.9-57.1cm (22-22.5in); bitches height 53.3-55.9cm (21-22in); weight 25-34kg (55-75lb)

Origin: native to Newfoundland and brought to Britain by fishermen in the early nineteenth century

Personality: hard-working, affectionate and lovable; a healthy, hardy dog

English setter

Description: an attractive and elegant dog, slender yet powerful looking

Head: lean, elongated with a well-defined stop; the muzzle is half the length of the head, with thickish lips and a tight jaw; the nose should be near-black.

Eyes: near hazel colour

Ears: should hang in neat folds

Tail: medium length, slightly curved and fringed; in line with the back

Body: of moderate length with a short, level back

Coat: slightly wavy, silky and moderately long with breeches and forelegs well feathered

Colour: preferred colouration is black and white; lemon and white; liver and white; or tricolour (black, white and red)

Sizes: dogs' height 55.9-68.6cm (22-27in); bitches' height 53.3-64.8cm (21-25.5in); weight 27-32kg (60-70lb)

Origin: obtained from the Spanish pointer and the French pointer, the English setter was developed via the French setter in the nineteenth century

Personality: friendly and affectionate, the English setter is also a sensitive dog and therefore receptive to good training

Gordon setter

Description: bigger and heavier than the English or Irish setters; more stylish, with the appearance of a thoroughbred

Head: a deep, slightly rounded head with more fully developed lips and a definite nasal stop

Eyes: brown

Ears: flat and slightly pointed

Tail: straight or below the line of the back, tapering from the root

Body: robust but of moderate length in all aspects

Coat: short and silky

Colour: deep shining black with mahogany markings; black pencilling on toes, white mark on chest, or black streak under the jaw are all admissible

Sizes: dogs' height 58.4-66cm (23-26in), bitches' height 55.9-62.2cm (22-24.5in); weight 24-33kg (53-72.5lb)

Origin: first bred at the end of the seventeenth century, at Gordon Castle in Banffshire, Scotland by the Scottish Duke Alexander IV of Gordon

Personality: a good willing dog to have around, never in the way; good sense of smell and a good retriever

Irish setter

Description: a handsome dog, more dashing than other setters

Head: long and lean with muzzle half the length of the head; straight nasal canal and nearly black nose

Eyes: hazel or dark brown

Ears: thin and soft to touch; almost triangular in shape

Tail: carried horizontally

Body: narrow-chested with a deep, somewhat streamlined thorax

Coat: long, flat and silky; short and fine on the head with feathering on the upper ears

Colour: rich mahogany without any trace of black

Sizes: dogs' height 53.3-61cm (21-24in), bitches' height 50.8-59.7cm (20-23.5in); dogs' weight 18-25kg (40-55lb), bitches' weight 15-22.3kg (33-49lb)

Origin: originally from Ireland, with Spanish pointer ancestry; possibly older than its English cousin

Personality: the Irish setter is a long-lived dog, and is both energetic and independent

Cocker spaniel

Description: a well-balanced compact dog, pleasing to look at

Head: a good square muzzle; rounded head; an upper lip that covers the lower jaw; strong teeth and well-developed nostrils

Eyes: various colours, depending on coat

Ears: long, wavy

Tail: set slightly lower than the line of the back

Body: compact and muscular, with strong neck; without dewlap

Coat: flat and silky-textured; of medium length with feathering but not wavy

Colour: solid black is most popular but also various other colours; white is only acceptable in self colours on the chest

Sizes: dogs' height 38.1cm (15in) maximum, bitches' height 35.5cm (14in) maximum; weight 10.9-12.7kg (24-28lb)

Origin: descended through careful breeding from the English cocker spaniel

Personality: happy companionable dogs, respectful and good with children

English cocker spaniel

Description: an elegant, hardy, sporting dog with a charming expression

Head: a square muzzle with a pronounced stop and a generous nose

Eyes: brown

Ears: set at eye level and hanging close to the ground, they need to be checked frequently and kept clear of ticks and burrs

Tail: set low, can be docked

Body: well-boned legs with solid round feet; the neck is muscular, set between sloping shoulders

Coat: silky and feathered but not wavy

Colour: many colours are allowed but white on the chest is only allowable in a solid-coloured dog

Sizes: dogs' height 39.3-40.6cm (15.5-16in), bitches' height 38.1-39.3cm (15-15.5in); weight 12.7-14.5kg (28-32lb)

Origin: all of the seven English spaniels have derived from a spaniel-type dog imported into Britain many centuries ago

Personality: a good companion, emotional and sensitive; bitches especially have a tendency to put on weight, so a controlled diet is essential; coats need frequent brushing

English springer spaniel

Description: a strong, compact dog, excellent in finding and springing game; more powerful and faster than the other British spaniels

Head: wide, slightly rounded head; well-developed nostrils and strong jaws

Eyes: dependent on coat colour, but hazel or brown most common

Ears: close to the head

Tail: docked in gun dog style

Body: long-legged, powerful dog with a strong, muscular neck

Coat: close, straight and of medium length, not coarse

Colour: most popular colours are the liver and white or black and white, especially with tan markings, but various other colours acceptable

Sizes: average height 50.8cm (20in); weight 22.2-24.1kg (49-53lb)

Origin: the oldest of the British gun dogs, and the founder of all British hunting spaniels

Personality: a cheerful, good-natured dog, the English springer spaniel is also prone to overweight and other characteristics are similar to those of the English cocker spaniel

Field spaniel

Description: looks very much like the cocker spaniel, but longer and lower

Head: a well-shaped, well-proportioned muzzle; important thinness below the eyes, and an open-nostrilled nose

Eyes: dark hazel or chestnut

Ears: longish and wide, fringed like those of a setter

Tail: fringed, and carried low

Body: a hardy, well-muscled body and neck; heavier than the cocker

Coat: slightly wavy

Colour: single coloured; either black, liver, golden/liver or mahogany red

Sizes: average height 45.7cm (18in); weight 15.9-22.7kg (35-50lb)

Origin: as with other cockers, via the English cocker and its Spanish origins

Personality: regarded as having the most pleasant of spaniel personalities, being both affectionate and intelligent; it is a good companionable dog

Irish water spaniel

Description: a compact, well-built and medium-sized dog

Head: rather large, with arched skull; muzzle is long and square in shape, with a large nose

Eyes: brown, small

Ears: long, hanging beside cheeks, well covered with ringlets

Tail: short, thick at the base and tapering to a point

Body: strong, thick neck tapers towards head; straight front legs, well-boned

Coat: curly coated with topknot in oily water-proof hair

Colour: deep liver with unique violet/purple tinge

Sizes: dogs' height 53.3-61cm (21-24in), bitches' height 50.8-58.4cm(20-23in); weight 25-27.3kg (55-60lb)

Origin: developed in the early nineteenth century in Ireland, with crossings which probably included the poodle and setter

Personality: obedient and intelligent, nervous of strangers. Their curly coats take a lot of work to keep clean. They have a great love of water; the ideal hunting dogs for marshes and lakes.

Sussex spaniel

Description: a strong, well-built spaniel, not as quick as either the cocker or springer, but a tireless worker

Head: well-balanced with a well-marked frontal stop

Eyes: hazel

Ears: lie close to the head; largish

Tail: docked to about 15cm (6in)

Body: a deep, well-developed chest and slightly arched neck

Coat: abundant hair, flat without curl, with a thick undercoat

Colour: golden liver — dark liver is not acceptable — with shading to gold at ends

Sizes: height 38-40.6cm (15-16in); dogs' weight up to 20kg (44lb), bitches' 18.2kg (40lb) maximum

Origin: first produced in the county of Sussex, England, from which it derives its name, at the beginning of the nineteenth century

Personality: quiet and thoughtful; energetic working, with a characteristic swinging gait; a good companionable dog

Welsh springer spaniel

Description: compactly built dog, slightly smaller than the English springer, and very hardy

Head: medium length, square muzzle; powerful jaws and a definite stop

Eyes: dark hazel

Ears: fringe covered, pendent type

Tail: low, never carried above the level of the back

Body: a muscular, strong body; not too long, with a deep brisket; a powerful neck, long and without dewlap

Coat: flat, thick and silky-textured; not wavy

Colour: white and bright red

Sizes: dogs' height 40.6-48.2cm (16-19in), bitches' height 38.1-45.7cm (15-18in); weight 15.9-20.4kg (35-45lb)

Origin: bred from spaniel stocks exclusively for hunting

Personality: a keen, hardworking and faithful dog, cheerful and yet quite independent

Belgian sheepdog (Groenendael)

Description: the best-known of the Belgian shepherds' dogs, taking its name from a town near Brussels; this is the long-haired black dog, the others being the fawn and charcoal short-haired and the ash-grey shaggy-haired
Head: finely chiselled, with muzzle half the length of the skull
Eyes: brown
Ears: triangular, small and erect
Tail: long and well-covered
Body: powerful but not bulky, with straight muscular legs
Coat: long, sleek and abundant; slightly thicker at the neck
Colour: black, with some white acceptable
Sizes: dogs' height 61-66cm (24-26in), bitches' height 56-61cm (22-24in); average weight 28.2kg (62lb)

Origin: the Belgian sheepdogs have been established for a very long time, with the Groenendael being isolated and recognised at the end of the nineteenth century

Personality: an excellent worker, easily trained; they make good herders and also good guard dogs, being suspicious of strangers but good with children

Border collie

Description: an untiring sheepdog, one of the best in the world
Head: a fairly broad skull, with blunted muzzle
Eyes: dark and alert
Ears: smallish, carried erect and the top half folding forward
Tail: carried low
Body: lithe, sturdy body; long in comparison to its straight legs
Coat: dense and of varied length
Colour: black and white; grey and white; red and white; black, white and tan; solid black or white
Sizes: dogs' height 45.7-55.9cm (18-22in), bitches' height 43.2-53.3cm (17-21in); dogs' weight 18.2-22.7kg (40-50lb), bitches' weight 15.9-20.5kg (35-45lb)

Origin: introduced to Scotland by Viking invaders, and crossed with the Valée sheepdog. Originally known as the Shepherds' Dog, it has also been called the English collie and the working collie, but is now recognised as the border collie.

Personality: very sensitive, intelligent dogs, bold and keen

Boxer

Description: a powerful dog, full of energy

Head: lean and in proportion to its body; with lower jaw extending beyond the upper jaw, not showing teeth or tongue when closed; the boxer also sports a large black nose with open nostrils

Eyes: dark

Ears: set high, docked to a point

Tail: short and carried high; in America and continental Europe, the boxer's tail is cropped, but left natural in the UK

Body: square-set; straight parallel front legs; a strong, round and muscular neck, no dewlap

Coat: the short coat lies close to the body and should be glossy

Colour: an essential black mask, together with fawn; brindle and fawn which is allowed in a range of shades from light yellow to deer red; white markings are also allowed

Sizes: dogs' height 55.9-63.5cm (22-25in), bitches' height 53.3-58.7cm (21-23.5in); dogs' weight 30-32.3kg (66-71lb), bitches' weight 24.1-25kg (53-55lb)

Origin: developed in the mid-nineteenth century in Munich, the German Boxer Club being formed in 1896

Personality: renowned for its great loyalty and protectiveness, good-natured; not long-lived

Bull mastiff

Description: a powerfully-built dog, but not cumbersome

Head: large square head; wrinkled, with a wide, open nose

Eyes: dark hazel

Ears: V-shaped, towards the back of the head and carried backwards

Tail: can be either straight or curved, and long enough to reach the hocks

Body: a short, straight back

Coat: short and hard to the touch

Colour: should be pure coloured, any shade of brindle, fawn or red

Sizes: dogs' height 63.5-68.6cm (25-27in), bitches' height 61-66cm (24-26in); dogs' weight 50-59kg (110-130lb), bitches' weight 41-54.5kg (90-120lb)

Origin: a cross between mastiffs and bulldogs, the breed first gained recognition in 1924

Personality: a highly-spirited dog, active and alert; necessitates a lot of exercise; a frightening bodyguard or watchdog

Rough collie

Description: a robust, handsome, active dog, still used as a sheepdog but also a guard dog, rescue dog and guide dog

Head: flat between the ears, with an elongated muzzle and a black nose

Eyes: dark, almond-shaped

Ears: small; not too close together; at the top of the skull

Tail: carried low with a slight lift at the end, which should reach its hocks

Body: long in comparison to height

Coat: dense and thick, especially at the collar

Colour: tricolour (tan, black and white); blue merle, sable and white

Sizes: dogs' height 55.9-66cm (22-26in), bitches' height 50.8-61cm (20-24in); dogs' weight 27.3-34.1kg (60-75lb), bitches' weight 22.7-29.6kg (50-65lb)

Origin: originally from Scotland, where they were used to guard the black-faced, black-footed colley sheep

Personality: kind, sensitive dogs but apt to be indolent and so must be trained most carefully; loyal and not aggressive, but suspicious of strangers

Dobermann Pinscher

Description: a powerful, elegant and stream-lined dog

Head: long; clean-cut; well filled under the eyes; a flat skull and an accentuated stop

Eyes: dark

Ears: docked and carried upright

Tail: docked quite short

Body: held in a proud carriage on perfectly straight legs

Coat: smooth; close-lying; a short, thick coat

Colour: black, brown or blue with rust markings

Sizes: dogs' height 66-71.1cm (26-28in); bitches' height 61-66cm (24-26in); weight 30-40kg (66-88lb)

Origin: the breed was created by Louis Dobermann towards the end of the nineteenth century, and improved upon by Otto Galler, who defined the breed which has been carefully controlled ever since

Personality: the ultimate watchdog, very loyal; the bitch is more tranquil and easy-going than the dog

German shepherd dog (Alsatian)

Description: above medium size, muscular and with a steady gait; can be either rough-coated, long rough-coated or long-haired

Head: in proportion to its body, long, lean and clean-cut; the back of the head is broad, with just a slight stop between the eyes; long muzzle with strong, powerful jaws

Eyes: dark and almond-shaped

Ears: wide at the base, pointed, upright and turned forwards

Tail: bushy, reaching almost to its hocks

Body: long-bodied, with a light but solid bone structure; muscular shoulders and front legs, and thick thighs

Coat: a medium-length double coat

Colour: black, grey; either may be uniform or have a shading of brown or yellow

Sizes: dogs' height 61-66cm (24-26in), bitches' height 55.9-61cm (22-24in); weight 35-38.6kg (77-85lb)

Origin: derived from the old herding and farm dogs of Germany, the Alsatian was popular by the end of the nineteenth century and made an invaluable contribution in both World Wars

Personality: obedient and loyal, the Alsatian is easily trained, being highly intelligent and courageous

Great Dane

Description: a giant, robust dog; very muscular and elegant

Head: long and narrow with an accentuated frontal stop and a large nasal canal

Eyes: mostly dark and round

Ears: long and pointed, carried erect; docked

Tail: medium length

Body: altogether graceful, with a long, muscular neck; perfectly straight long legs and muscular thighs

Coat: short and dense, with a sleek appearance to the close-lying hair

Colour: brindle; fawn; black, blue or harlequin, with a pure white underground with blue or black patches

Sizes: dogs' height 76.2cm (30in) minimum, bitches' height 71.1cm (28in) minimum; dogs' weight 54.4kg (120lb) minimum, bitches' weight 45.5kg (100lb) minimum

Origin: of very ancient lineage, the German mastiff (as it is known in Germany) was used for hunting stags and boars. The Great Dane Club was formed in Britain in 1883.

Personality: patient and affectionate, yet they can be aggressive when called upon; they make impressive companions

Mastiff

Description: a large, massive and powerful dog which, in the past, was a ferocious fighter

Head: heavy, wide head; well-developed and rectangular in shape, with slightly pendent lips; a large black nose and black muzzle

Eyes: small, dark hazel

Ears: rounded, set high; black

Tail: long, reaching down to the hocks

Body: a sturdy frame, with solid muscled shoulders; a wide chest and a thick powerful neck

Coat: short, thick hair

Colour: fawn, either golden or light, silver or apricot

Sizes: dogs' height 76.2cm (30in) minimum, bitches' height 69.8cm (27.5in) minimum; weight 79.5-86.4kg (175-190lb)

Origin: descended from the Tibetan mastiff, and introduced into Europe by the Phoenicians

Personality: the great care taken in breeding has eliminated the mastiff's natural ferocity, and a more gentle and good-natured dog is the result, but one that is still a highly competent guard dog

Old English sheepdog

Description: compact and very strong, the dog has great symmetry and a lot of coat

Head: the skull is large and square, the stop well-defined

Eyes: dark

Ears: small and lying flat against the head

Tail: tailless; any pups born with tails should be docked

Body: stocky, with a surprisingly long gait when galloping

Coat: thick, hard-textured, needing frequent brushing to avoid snarls; not curled

Colour: any shade of grey, grizzled blue or blue merle; white markings are acceptable

Sizes: dogs' height 55.9cm (22in) on average, bitches' slightly less; weight 30kg (66lb) average

Origin: the sheepdog's ancestry is not certain, but it was developed in the West Country of England

Personality: a good companionable dog, good with children; in addition, the Old English sheepdog is an excellent herder and a good guard dog

Pyrenean mountain dog

Description: a very big, strong and well-balanced dog, with an elegant movement

Head: large, bear-like with a wide, slightly pointed muzzle

Eyes: brown

Ears: small, triangular in shape, and pendent

Tail: long and well-covered, it rolls up when the dog is excited

Body: a strong, thick body and neck; straight front legs and well-muscled hindquarters

Coat: coarse-textured, thick outer coat which can be slightly wavy but not curly, and a substantial undercoat of fine hairs

Colour: white or mainly white with patches of light tan, grey or badger

Sizes: dogs' height 68.6-81.3cm (27-32in); bitches' height 63.5-73.6cm (25-29in); weight 40.9-56.8kg (90-125lb); dogs can be bigger, provided they comply to type

Origin: descended from the Hungarian kuvasz and the Maremma sheepdog

Personality: a real mountain dog, obedient and hard-working; easily trained and a good guide or rescue dog; loves open space but will adapt to family life

Rottweiler

Description: one of the foremost working breeds, of above average size; strong and sturdy

Head: big and round with a well-developed muzzle and scissor bite

Eyes: dark brown

Ears: triangular in shape; set wide apart and carried forwards

Tail: can be docked if too long

Body: broad, deeply-chested powerful dog

Coat: hard hair, thick and flat with an undercoat which should not show

Colour: black, with clearly-defined markings to the legs, chest, muzzle, eyes and beneath the tail

Sizes: dogs' height 61-68.6cm (24-27in), bitches' height 58.4-63.5cm (23-25in); weight 50kg (110lb) average

Origin: descended possibly from the Italian mastiffs in the Middle Ages, and bred in Germany, where it finally gained popularity in the early twentieth century

Personality: obedient and brave; an excellent guard dog that will protect its owner; easy to train

St Bernard

Description: a very large, powerful dog, robust and muscular

Head: massive, wide head with very wrinkled skin; a straight nasal canal and a pronounced stop; drooping upper lips

Eyes: sited towards the front of the head; dark brown in colour and of medium size

Ears: medium-sized, pendent ears that fall sideways

Tail: large, well-covered and reaching down to the hocks

Body: heavily-built, strong and highly enduring

Coat: of medium length and skimpy; it needs frequent grooming; it can be slightly wavy but not curly

Colour: any shade of red, with white markings

Sizes: dogs' height 69.8cm (27.5in) minimum (the bigger the better), bitches' height 64.7cm (25.5in); weight 50-55kg (110-121lb)

Origin: thought to have been introduced to the Alps by the Romans and to have descended from the Tibetan mastiff; it appeared in about the year 1000, in the Hospice of St Bernard the Menthon

Personality: world-famous for their rescuing feats in the Alps, today basically a companionable dog but one unsuited to apartment life as it is in need of a good deal of exercise

Samoyed

Description: the Samoyed is a beautiful strong, active dog; an excellent sledge dog, able to pull heavy loads long distances

Head: a powerful wedge-shaped head with strong jaws and a black or brown nose

Eyes: dark

Ears: slightly rounded, of medium size; erect

Tail: long and fully-covered; carried rolled on the back

Body: strong, square body with solid muscular legs and flat feet

Coat: a thick soft undercoat, which provides insulation, and a thick harsh outer coat which should not be wavy

Colour: pure white is preferred, but off-white, yellow, and white and yellow are also accepted

Sizes: dogs' height 50.8-59.7cm (20-23.5in), bitches' height 45.7-53.3cm (18-21in); weight 22.7-29.6kg (50-65lb)

Origin: the dog takes its name from the Siberian Samoyed tribe of hunters and fishermen, who used such a dog for centuries. It was introduced to England at the end of the nineteenth century.

Personality: a peaceful, gentle and obedient dog; an excellent companion and watchdog. The Samoyed has a reputation for cleanliness and also for frequent barking.

Siberian husky

Description: a medium-sized, lightweight yet robust dog, capable of travelling very long distances pulling laden sledges, often in very low temperatures

Head: a wolf-like, long and lean face with a black nose

Eyes: brown or light blue

Ears: erect and set high on the head

Tail: round and well-covered, it is usually carried curved over the back

Body: quite compact, and well covered in fur; a beautiful effortless gait; feet are slightly webbed

Coat: a double coat, as necessitated by the climate; woolly underneath and a soft outer coat

Colour: all colours and all markings are acceptable

Sizes: dogs' height 53.3-59.7cm (21-23.5in), bitches' height 50.8-55.9cm (20-22in); dogs' weight 20.45-27.27kg (45-60lb), bitches' weight 15.8-22.7kg (35-50lb)

Origin: a native of Siberia, it was introduced into Alaska at the beginning of the twentieth century

Personality: gentle and friendly, the husky is easy to train and provides good company but is also easily bored

Welsh corgi

Description: there are two varieties of Welsh corgi, the Cardigan and the Pembroke; both are sturdy, low-set dogs

Head: foxy in expression, with a large flat skull

Eyes: hazel

Ears: of medium size, held erect; ends rounded

Tail: the Cardigan's is moderately long, set in line with the body; the Pembroke has virtually no tail at all

Body: long, round body with deep chest on very short legs

Coat: the Cardigan has short, hard hairs; the Pembroke has hair of medium length, not wiry

Colour: any colour is acceptable, with the exception of pure white, for the Cardigan; for the Pembroke, self colours of red, sable, fawn, black and tan are all acceptable, and it may have white markings

Sizes: height 25.4-30.5cm (10-12in); dogs' weight 9.1-10.9kg (20-24lb), bitches' weight 8.2-10kg (18-22lb)

Origin: believed to have derived from Flemish dwarf dogs brought to England at the beginning of the twelfth century, crossed with native Welsh dogs

Personality: a lively, spirited dog; an energetic sheep dog and an intelligent, pleasant companion

Airedale terrier

Description: the largest of the terriers; very smart

Head: long, flat skull; not too broad between the ears; elongated muzzle

Eyes: small; dark

Ears: small, V-shaped and carried semi-erect

Tail: docked and carried high

Body: parallel, straight front legs; chest not wide, producing a deep narrow body

Coat: hard wiry coat, not too long but dense and resistant to dampness

Colour: tan with black or dark grizzle body

Sizes: dogs' height 58.4-61cm (23-24in), bitches' height 55.9-58.4cm (22-23in); weight 20kg (44lb) average

Origin: thought to be the result of breeding between the English terrier and the otterhound, first carried out in Yorkshire, England

Personality: patient, lively dog; very affectionate and intelligent; the Airedale was used extensively during World War I by the Army.

Australian terrier

Description: low set, compact dog; active and vivacious
Head: a long head with powerful jaws and a black nose
Eyes: small and dark
Ears: small, pointed ears held erect
Tail: docked
Body: short-legged with rather a long neck in comparison
Coat: hard straight hair, 5-7.5cm (2-3in) in length
Colour: blue, black or silver/grey body with tan on legs and face; the Australian terrier also has a topknot of blue or silver; alternatively, it may be a clear sandy – light or reddish – colour
Sizes: height 25cm (10in) average; weight 4.5-6.4kg (10-14lb)

Origin: bred in Australia by careful inter-breeding of terriers including Scottish, fox, Skye, cairn, Yorkshire and Dandie Dinmont

Personality: a highly-spirited dog, very affectionate and a good companion

Border terrier

Description: the smallest of the terriers; nimble, robust and active
Head: otterlike in appearance, with a short sturdy muzzle
Eyes: dark
Ears: small; V-shaped; falling forward over the cheeks
Tail: thick; not docked; natural but not long
Body: deep and narrow; long in comparison to the legs, with the ribcage well back
Coat: thick and dense topcoat, and also a thick undercoat
Colour: red; wheaten; grizzle and tan or blue and tan
Sizes: height 25cm (10in) approximately; dogs' weight 6-7kg (13.2-15.4lb), bitches' weight 5-6kg (11-13.2lb)

Origin: bred in the Border regions between England and Scotland, for going to ground after foxes

Personality: bold and lively; well adapted to the home and good with children

Bull terrier

Description: very strongly built; very muscular dog, bred to fight

Head: a long, deep head; very strong ovoid in shape, when viewed head-on; without stop

Eyes: small, dark and almond-shaped

Ears: set well back on the head; erect, triangular and pointed

Tail: carried horizontally; thick at the base, tapering to a point

Body: full, round-bodied with robust muscular shoulders

Coat: short, hard, shiny hairs

Colour: split into two groups for shows; pure white, and coloured

Sizes: height 50.8-53.3cm (20-21in); weight 23.4-28.18kg (52-62lb)

Origin: bulldogs crossed with terriers, plus some pointer blood

Personality: a loyal, obedient dog, that has lost its original ferocious fighting qualities though they still make excellent guard dogs

Cairn terrier

Description: a small, foxy terrier; shaggy in appearance

Head: small with a broad skull and an indentation between the eyes; a powerful but not heavy muzzle

Eyes: deep-set; dark hazel

Ears: carried erect; pointed

Tail: carried jauntily

Body: small and well-proportioned with short, well-boned legs

Coat: double-coated, with a hard, not coarse, and plentiful outer coat and a soft, short fur-like undercoat

Colour: red; sandy; grey; brindled or near-black; black and white is not accepted

Sizes: height up to 30cm (12in); weight 6.4kg (14lb)

Origin: established for a very long time in Scotland, and employed to ferret out small animals in addition to foxes and badgers from their dens

Personality: a lively, affectionate dog that has converted readily to become a good companion, well-suited to life in the apartment

Dandie Dinmont

Description: long-bodied; short-legged; with a 'toupée' on its head
Head: large and solid, with a black nose
Eyes: radiant and lively
Ears: pendent
Tail: from 20-25cm (7.9-9.8in) long
Body: long and flexible, with muscular thighs and short legs; the back curves downwards over the shoulders, with an arch over the loin
Coat: the hair must be about 5cm (2in) long, and a mixture of hard and soft
Colour: shades of pepper or mustard
Sizes: height 20.3-27.9cm (8-11in); weight 8.2-10.9kg (18-24lb)

Origin: an old breed of crossed terriers from the borders of England and Scotland; it takes its name from a Walter Scott character, a sporting farmer who owned a pack of them

Personality: playful and affectionate, the Dandie Dinmont is a good companion

Fox terrier (wire-haired)

Description: well-proportioned, elegant dog

Head: slightly chiselled, otherwise wedge-shaped

Eyes: dark and character-revealing

Ears: small; V-shaped, the flaps folding over neatly and dropping forward to lie against the cheeks

Tail: should be docked

Body: powerful for its size, with every aspect in good proportion

Coat: dense, shaggy, but not too curly

Colour: brown or black markings on a white background

Sizes: height 39.4cm (15.5in) maximum; weight 8kg (17.6lb)

Origin: a long-established breed, with its origin dating back to ancient times in the smooth-haired fox terrier

Personality: lively, active and playful; the fox terrier uses up a lot of energy, and does a lot of barking; they have a tendency to be jealous but not spiteful.

Irish terrier

Description: a close relation to the wire-haired fox terrier, this is a courageous and dignified dog

Head: long, with a flat skull narrow between the ears; an elongated muzzle with muscular jaws

Eyes: small, dark and not too prominent

Ears: V-shaped and quite small, folding forward

Tail: docked, carried erect

Body: strong, muscular body; well-boned, with straight front legs

Coat: hard and wiry; definitely not soft or curly

Colour: red; either a bright, wheaten or yellow shade

Sizes: height 45.7cm (18in) average; dogs' weight 12kg (26.4lb), bitches' weight 11kg (24.2lb)

Origin: a very old breed, which first appeared in paintings at the beginning of the eighteenth century

Personality: a kind, affectionate dog; easy to train

Jack Russell terrier

Description: a strain of wire-haired fox terrier, able to run with hounds or go to ground
Head: strongly-boned, with powerful jaws and strong cheek muscles
Eyes: almond-shaped, deep-set and dark
Ears: small, V-shaped, drop forward close to the head
Tail: set high
Body: a straight back, with strong angular hind-quarters and short legs
Coat: smooth or broken-coated, definitely not woolly
Colour: white with markings in tan, black or traditional hound colours
Sizes: height up to 28cm (11in); there is another sized Jack Russell, the height of which is between 28-38cm (11-15in)

Origin: developed in the nineteenth century by the Rev John Russell, the breed is still not recognised by either the English or the American Kennel Club, although a standard has now been drawn up

Personality: a courageous dog; its obedience makes it a good companion

Lakeland terrier

Description: a small, distinguished, workman-like terrier

Head: well-balanced, elongated head with a flat skull

Eyes: dark or hazel

Ears: V-shaped, small ears that drop forward

Tail: should be carried high but not curled over the back

Body: straight, strongly-boned legs

Coat: rough, weather-resistant and dense, with an undercoat

Colour: black and tan; blue and tan; red; wheaten; red grizzle; liver; blue or black; white markings on feet and chest are also acceptable

Sizes: height 36.8cm (14.5in) maximum; dogs' weight 7.7kg (17lb), bitches' weight 6.8kg (15lb)

Origin: originally known as the Patterdale terrier, it was perfected in the English Lake District, in the nineteenth century

Personality: fearless, cheerful and affectionate, the Lakeland terrier can also be very stubborn

Norfolk terrier

Description: one of the smaller terriers, fearless, hyperactive and full of stamina

Head: wide skull with a slightly rounded and well-defined stop; the Norfolk has a foxy appearance, with a strong muzzle

Eyes: dark and lively

Ears: hanging tight to the cheek

Tail: docked to half length

Body: straight, strong front legs and muscular back legs

Coat: hard, straight and wiry, lying close to the body, with longer hair round the neck and shoulders

Colour: red in various shades; black and tan, or grizzle

Sizes: height 25.4cm (10in); weight 4.5-5.5kg (10-12lb)

Origin: originally from the English county of Norfolk, since 1964 it has become recognised as a separate breed, distinct from the Norwich terrier

Personality: well-adapted to the apartment, devoid of nerves, affectionate and active

Norwich terrier

Description: a small, joyful terrier with a hardy constitution and a fearless temperament

Head: like the Norfolk, with black nose and large menacing teeth

Eyes: dark, expressive

Ears: set well apart on the top of the skull; the Norwich differs from the Norfolk in that the ears are carried erect and are of medium size, and pointed

Tail: docked to half length

Body: compact body with short, strongly-boned legs

Coat: hard, straight and wiry; lies close to the body and is short and shiny on the head and muzzle

Colour: red in various shades; black and tan, or grizzle

Sizes: height 25.4cm (10in); weight 4.5-5.5kg (10-12lb)

Origin: a long-established breed, admitted to the English Kennel Club in 1932; the drop-eared Norfolk is now separately recognised

Personality: the Norfolk and Norwich are basically identical, lovable companions, well-adapted to living with young energetic people

Scottish terrier

Description: a vigorous, thickset, sturdy and compact dog

Head: long and narrow, with a large nose and teeth; a definite stop between skull and muzzle

Eyes: dark brown, almond-shaped

Ears: erect and smooth, pointed

Tail: of medium length, carried either straight or slightly curved

Body: short legs; powerful muscular neck

Coat: a harsh, dense and wiry outer coat over a soft, short, dense undercoat which acts as protection against adverse weather

Colour: black, wheaten or brindle

Sizes: height 25.4-27.9cm (10-11in); weight 8.6-10.5kg (19-23lb)

Origin: originally known as the Aberdeen terrier, the Scottish terrier was registered as a separate breed with the Kennel Club at the end of the nineteenth century.

Personality: lively and proud, the Scottish terrier is a dignified dog, showing a great deal of affection towards members of its human family.

Sealyham terrier

Description: a most beautiful, free-moving active dog

Head: slightly domed and wide between the ears; powerful jaws and a large nose

Eyes: dark, round and of medium size

Ears: wide and carried against the cheeks

Tail: docked and carried upright

Body: a long, muscular neck; short, straight front legs; powerful, muscular hind legs

Coat: long, coarse and bristly with a long beard

Colour: white; white with lemon, brown or badger pied markings on head and ears

Sizes: height 30.5cm (12in) maximum; dogs' weight 9.1kg (20lb), bitches' weight 8.2kg (18lb)

Origin: developed from the middle of the nineteenth century by Captain John Edwards in Sealyham, Wales and recognised by the English Kennel Club in 1910.

Personality: an aristocratic, cheerful terrier, full of spirited affection and a good companion

Skye terrier

Description: this terrier's length should be twice its height

Head: a long head with powerful jaws and a black nose

Eyes: dark brown

Ears: can be pricked or dropped, and always black

Tail: pendent; should not be curled

Body: a typically purebred short-legged terrier with straight back and well-proportioned muscular neck

Coat: a long, hard top coat flat against the body, and without curl, over a short, softly woolly undercoat

Colour: dark or light grey; fawn, cream or black

Sizes: height 25.4cm (10in); dogs' weight 11.4kg (25lb), bitches' weight 10.2kg (22.5lb)

Origin: bred from local terriers and Maltese dogs, the Skye terrier has not changed since the beginning of the seventeenth century.

Personality: distrustful of strangers, but excessively loyal to its master; immortalised as Greyfriars Bobby, the Edinburgh dog which lived by its master's grave for ten years.

Staffordshire bull terrier

Description: a strong, muscular, square-set dog

Head: short, with a broad skull and pronounced cheek muscles; a distinct stop, short foreface and black nose

Eyes: round and dark

Ears: semi-erect

Tail: medium length, set low; should not be curled

Body: broad, deep chest with a short, muscular neck

Coat: smooth, short, soft hairs that lie tight to the body

Colour: red; fawn; white; black; blue, or any of these colours with white; brindle in various shades or with white

Sizes: 35.6-40.6cm (14-16in); dogs' weight 12.7-17.3kg (28-38lb), bitches' weight 10.9-15kg (24-33lb)

Origin: a cross between bulldog and terrier, which was recognised by both the English and the American Kennel Clubs in 1935. In America, the name was altered to American Staffordshire terrier, and the breed is heavier than in Europe.

Personality: tenacious and courageous; the Staffordshire bull terrier is affectionate both to friends and to children

Welsh terrier

Description: a robust and hardy working terrier, with a quizzical expression; the Welsh terrier looks like a miniature Airedale

Head: long, with a deeper muzzle than the fox terrier; a powerful jaw and strong teeth; the nose is black

Eyes: small, dark

Ears: set fairly high; V-shaped, small and carried forward

Tail: docked, carried high

Body: straight, muscular limbs with small round cat-like feet

Coat: rough full coat, hard to the touch

Colour: black and tan; black grizzle and tan; black below the hocks is not acceptable

Sizes: height 39.4cm (15.5in) maximum at the shoulder; weight 9.1-9.5kg (20-21lb)

Origin: an old breed, established as a wire-haired terrier and descending from the English Black terrier; it came to prominence at the end of the nineteenth century

Personality: obedient and easily trained, the Welsh terrier is affectionate and lively

West Highland White terrier

Description: small, hardy terrier; confident, strong and agile
Head: slightly convexly curved skull; a pronounced stop and short, closely-fitting jaws
Eyes: dark, deep, set wide apart
Ears: small, erect
Tail: 12.7-15.3cm (6-7in) long; not docked; carried erect
Body: deep-chested with muscular legs
Coat: double-coated; the outer coat should not be curled, and should be about 5cm (2in) long
Colour: pure white
Sizes: height 27.9-30.5cm (11-12in); weight 6.8-10kg (15-22lb)

Origin: white pups from a litter of Cairn terriers in Argyll, Scotland, were selected and bred to produce the West Highland White at the end of the nineteenth century.

Personality: this spirited little dog is companionable and well-adapted to apartment life; it likes to be active and enjoys roaming about

Cavalier King Charles spaniel

Description: a good-looking and well-proportioned dog, with a sporting nature
Head: almost flat between the ears without dome; long muzzle and shallow stop; open nostrils
Eyes: dark, prominent
Ears: long, set quite high
Tail: medium length, can be docked
Body: nicely proportioned, with bony front legs and angular thighs
Coat: long, silky and free from curl, with feathering on ears, tail and legs
Colour: black and tan; ruby; Blenheim and tricolour (black, white and chestnut)
Sizes: height 30.5-33cm (12-13in); weight 5.5-8.6kg (12-19lb)

Origin: originating from the same stock as the English Toy spaniel, the breed was established in 1926, when an American, Roswell Eldridge, offered a prize at Crufts for a class of old-type Blenheim spaniels. The breed was finally registered with the English Kennel Club in 1945.

Personality: pleasant, active and companionable; a genuinely amiable dog

Chihuahua (smooth coat)

Description: one of the most popular toy dogs, the Chihuahua is regarded as the smallest dog in the world

Head: an apple-domed skull, with an area known as a molero where the skull bones do not join; short, pointed muzzle

Eyes: very black and round

Ears: large and when the dog is alert, held erect

Tail: carried curved, either over the back or to the side

Body: small and compact, longer than its height

Coat: smooth and soft, with a glossy appearance

Colour: any plain colour or mixture

Sizes: height 15.2-22.8cm (6-9in); weight, ideally below 2.7kg (6lb); the smaller dogs are preferable

Origin: of Mexican origin, descended from the Aztecs' sacred dog and developed in America from the beginning of the twentieth century

Personality: a very active dog, with a cheeky expression; loyal and affectionate, an ideal companion dog for the apartment, provided it is given plenty of exercise

English Toy terrier
(Black and Tan)

Description: a miniature form of the Manchester terrier
Head: long and narrow, with a flat skull
Eyes: dark, protruding
Ears: pear-shaped, placed well back on the skull, pointed at the tops and carried erect
Tail: sturdy, slightly docked
Body: well-proportioned, with a full, wide chest
Coat: thick, close and smooth, with a glossy appearance
Colour: black or black with clearly-defined tan on the forelegs, muzzle, throat, inside of hind legs and under the tail
Sizes: height 25.4cm (10in); weight 2.7-3.6kg (6-8lb)

Origin: obtained by repeated crossings of small Manchester terriers; the breed became known as Toy Black and Tans before being recognised by the English Kennel Club as English Toy terriers (Black and Tan) in 1962

Personality: fearless and affectionate; these little dogs, which are one of the smallest known breeds, are excellent companions

Griffin Bruxellois

Description: small, rough-coated terrier with a monkey-like expression
Head: large and round, with a deep stop between nose and skull; a prominent chin, and visible teeth; black nose
Eyes: large, round and black
Ears: upright, docked to a point
Tail: docked to two-thirds of its length, and carried high
Body: square-set; well-balanced, with a strong neck and deep chest
Coat: harsh and wiry, without curl; quite dishevelled
Colour: red; black, or black and tan
Sizes: height 17.8-20.3cm (7-8in); weight not more than 3kg (6.6lb) for the smaller variety and not more than 5kg (11lb) for the larger
Origin: imported from Belgium to Britain, where they were crossed with the Yorkshire, miniature schnauzer and the pug

Personality: lively and intelligent, full of character; they are both curious and moody, and very free with their barking

Italian greyhound

Description: a miniature greyhound, graceful and elegant with a high-stepping action

Head: long, flat and narrow, with a very fine muzzle; dark nose and thin lips

Eyes: dark, large

Ears: placed well back, rose-shaped

Tail: straight, ending with a slight curve

Body: a curved back, drooping at the hindquarters; altogether a slender, finely-boned body and long, thin neck

Coat: fine, thick and glossy hair

Colour: various shades of fawn; white; cream; blue or black; white paws or chest are also acceptable

Sizes: height 33-38.1cm (13-15in); weight 5kg (11lb) maximum

Origin: of very ancient origin, dating back to Egyptian times; developed in Italy and imported into Britain at the beginning of the seventeenth century

Personality: well-behaved; almost a timid dog, peaceful and devoted; requires gentle handling; not suited to a boisterous environment

Japanese Chin

Description: a dainty, decorative dog with a continual look of astonishment on its face

Head: a broad skull, rounded at the front; open nostrils with a short nasal canal, a short muzzle and distinct stop

Eyes: dark and almond-shaped, with the white showing in the inner corners

Ears: inverted V-shape, and well covered with hair

Tail: falls onto its back

Body: distinctively dainty; the smaller the better

Coat: profuse, long and straight with a soft, silky texture

Colour: black and white or red and white

Sizes: height 22.8cm (9in) maximum; weight 3.2kg (7lb) minimum

Origin: probably originally from Korea, but developed in Japan as the Japanese spaniel, spreading to Europe at the beginning of the eighteenth century

Personality: docile and devoted; bred purely as a companion dog; the Chin is susceptible to distemper

King Charles spaniel

Description: a compact, cobby dog; smaller than the Cavalier

Head: a large, well-domed skull, full over the eyes; short, upturned nose and a deep stop

Eyes: dark and large

Ears: long, feathered and hanging on the cheeks

Tail: well-flagged and carried low

Body: wide, deep chest and short, straight back; short, straight legs

Coat: long, straight and silky, with feathering to the limbs

Colour: the four varieties of King Charles are determined by colour; the real King Charles is black and bright fawn. The Ruby is chestnut red, the Blenheim is red and white, and the tricolour form in white, tan and black is the Prince Charles.

Sizes: height 25.4cm (10in); weight 3.6-6.4kg (8-14lb)

Origin: now declining in numbers, it reached its popularity peak in the Edwardian era; its actual origins are not known.

Personality: a timorous companion dog, needing little exercise

Löwchen

Description: known as the little lion dog, because of the clipped rear half and upper legs of the dog, which leaves a ruff-like collar; a plumed tail and feathered feet

Head: short head with a broad skull and black nose

Eyes: round, very dark

Ears: pendent, feathered

Tail: tipped with a plume; the tail is of medium length

Body: short and well-proportioned

Coat: long and wavy, the body should be clipped like a toy poodle from the middle of the body to the rear

Colour: white, black or lemon

Sizes: height 20.3-35.6cm (8-14in); weight 2-4.1kg (4.5-9lb)

Origin: originating in southern Europe, it is regarded as the rarest purebred dog in the world

Personality: an intelligent little dog, that makes an excellent companion

Maltese

Description: a toy breed completely enveloped in long, luxuriant silky hair

Head: well-balanced, with a pure black nose; the muzzle length should be one-third of the total head length

Eyes: dark brown, with black eye rings

Ears: pendent, heavily covered in hair

Tail: feathered and arched over the back

Body: short, cobby body; a straight back

Coat: good, straight, long, beautiful hair, about 22cm (8.7in) long

Colour: pure white, slight lemon colouration is sometimes allowed

Sizes: dogs' height 20.3-25.4cm (8-10in), bitches' height 20.3-22.8cm (8-9in); weight 3-4kg (6.6-8.8lb)

Origin: the oldest of the European toy breeds, it has been prominent in Malta for hundreds of years and developed in Italy with cross-breeding which introduced poodle and miniature spaniel blood

Personality: charming and sweet-natured, the Maltese is an intelligent dog and very lovable

Papillon

Description: a dainty, well-balanced dog; the ears resemble butterflies' wings, from which it derives its name (*papillon* is French for butterfly)
Head: a light head, with extended stop and slightly flat, black nose
Eyes: wide and dark
Ears: carried erect, wide open and turned to the sides; the insides of the ears are covered by fine wavy hair
Tail: medium length; well-covered, and carried curled over the back
Body: should be slightly longer than its height
Coat: fine, abundant, wavy, long and silky
Colour: white with patches which may be any colour except liver
Sizes: 20.3-27.9cm (8-11in); weight 4.1-4.5kg (9-10lb)

Origin: initially known as the dwarf spaniel in southern Europe

Personality: an adaptable dog, which makes for a charming companion; they are intelligent, obedient and not given to excessive barking

Pekingese

Description: a small, well-balanced and thick-set dog

Head: a large, broad skull, flat and wide between the ears; short, broad nose with large nostrils, a wrinkled muzzle and a deep stop

Eyes: large, dark

Ears: heart-shaped, with long feathering

Tail: set high and carried slightly curved over the back; with very long feathering

Body: short, with a short, thick neck; large flat feet with the front feet turned slightly out

Coat: long, straight hair, with a large mane extending well beyond the shoulders

Colour: all colours are permissible

Sizes: height 15.2-22.8cm (6-9in); dogs' weight not over 5kg (11lb), bitches' weight not over 5.5kg (12lb)

Origin: lost in the ancient history of its native China; the Pekingese was introduced to Europe in 1860, following discovery of these dogs in the ruins of the Summer Palace by French and British soldiers

Personality: the epitome of the lap dog, they need frequent combing; the teeth should be regularly cleaned to avoid their premature loss

Pomeranian

Description: a compact, short little dog with a foxy look and a big frill around the collar
Head: wedge-shaped, with black nose; ears set wide apart
Eyes: small, dark
Ears: pointed, upright
Tail: turned straight over the back and carried flat; abundantly covered in long, spreading hairs
Body: short, with well-rounded ribs
Coat: double-coated; the undercoat is short and fluffy, the outer comprised of long straight hair which is in abundance around the neck
Colour: any colour is acceptable, but must be free from black or white shadings
Sizes: height 30.5cm (12in) maximum; weight 5kg (11lb) maximum

Origin: a member of the spitz family, originating in the Arctic; developed in the Prussian region of Pomerania and introduced into Britain at the end of the nineteenth century
Personality: very apt to bark at strangers and therefore a good watchdog; they are lively, yet obedient

Poodle (toy)

Description: in every way a replica of the standard and miniature, apart from its size; the poodle has become one of the most popular dogs throughout the world

Head: proportionate to its body; rectilinear in shape; black nose or brown; flat cheeks and scissors bite

Eyes: black or brown

Ears: falling down against the cheeks, well covered in wavy hair

Tail: set high; docked

Body: neat and well-proportioned in every respect

Coat: curly, clipped most commonly in the accepted styles of puppy clip, English saddle clip or continental clip

Colour: single coloured black; white; blue; grey; silver; cream, brown or *café-au-lait*

Sizes: height below 27.9cm (11in) for the English Kennel Club; 25.4cm (10in) in America

Origin: bred down from the miniature poodle, the toy has the same origins as the standard poodle; the toy was granted separate recognition in the 1950s

Personality: good-natured and cheerful companions

Pug

Description: a compact, square-set and very muscular dog

Head: very large, round head with a short square muzzle and deep frown-like wrinkles on the forehead

Eyes: dark, prominent

Ears: pendent and silky, soft

Tail: tightly curled over the haunches

Body: straight, strong limbs and a well-developed muscular body

Coat: fine, soft, short and glossy

Colour: silver, apricot-yellow or black; the ears and mask should be as dark as possible, and clearly defined

Sizes: height 25.4-27.9cm (10-11in); weight 6.4-8.2kg (14-18lb)

Origin: they were introduced into Holland from China at the end of the sixteenth century, and the breed was later perfected in Britain

Personality: an affectionate and loyal dog, making a good companion. They become extremely uncomfortable in very hot weather.

Yorkshire terrier

Description: very good-looking, the Yorkie is the most popular toy dog in the UK

Head: small, flat with a medium-length muzzle and a black nose

Eyes: dark

Ears: small, V-shaped; can be erect or semi-erect

Tail: docked to a medium length and carried level with the back

Body: well-proportioned, with an upright carriage; straight limbs and round feet

Coat: long, straight, silky hair with a parting running from the nose to the end of the tail

Colour: steel blue with golden areas to the head, chest and limbs; abundant at the head, but not extending onto the neck and darker at the roots than in the middle

Sizes: height 22.8cm (9in); weight up to 3.2kg (7lb)

Origin: developed by miners in the English county of Yorkshire as a ratter; today's standard first appeared at show in 1870

Personality: this little terrier is lively and stubborn; happy both indoors and outside, shows great affection to its master but not to other animals

Boston terrier

Description: a compact dog of medium size, sturdy and muscular

Head: the skull is square, flat at the top with a well-defined stop; short muzzle; flat cheeks and a large black nose

Eyes: dark, set well apart, large and round

Ears: carried erect, the ears are small and fine

Tail: short, carried low

Body: broad-chested with straight muscular limbs and a slightly arched neck

Coat: short, smooth and of fine texture

Colour: brindle with white markings to head, chest, feet and tail

Sizes: height 38.1-43.1cm (15-17in); weight varies considerably, up to 11.4kg (25lb)

Origin: bred in America, the Boston terrier is the result of crossings between English bulldogs and white English terriers in the second half of the nineteenth century

Personality: an affectionate and patient companion; alert, intelligent and well-behaved

Bulldog

Description: a compact, thick-set dog; broad, powerful and beautifully ugly

Head: massive; large head in proportion to its body; an undershot jaw projecting beyond the upper jaw and cheeks extending to the sides of the eyes. The face should be full of deep folds, with a broad black nose and large nostrils

Eyes: round and very dark

Ears: small, thin, folded like rose petals

Tail: short and carried low

Body: an arched neck with dewlap; short legs; wide-chested

Coat: fine-textured, short and close

Colour: any colour is permissible, except black or black and tan

Sizes: height 30.5-35.6cm (12-14in); dogs' weight 24.1-25kg (53-55lb), bitches' weight 22.3-23.2kg (49-51lb)

Origin: a descendent of the ancient Asiatic mastiff, it was developed in medieval Britain

Personality: a charming and good-natured dog, but tenacious when roused

Chow Chow

Description: a member of the Spitz family, well-balanced and with a leonine appearance

Head: broad, with a flat skull; muzzle broad near the eyes, narrowing towards the black nose but not pointed; it is important that the tongue, gums and lips are purple

Eyes: small and dark

Ears: triangular, carried erect and turned forward

Tail: carried well over the back

Body: broad, deep chest; short kidney area, producing a short-coupled dog; hocks are straight, with no angulation

Coat: double-coated, with soft woolly undercoat and a coarse outer coat, long over neck, shoulders and nape, forming a thick mane

Colour: single coloured; black; red; fawn; blue, cream or white; the white is quite rare; markings are not acceptable

Sizes: height 45.7-50.8cm (18-20in); weight 25-27.3kg (55-60lb)

Origin: an ancient Chinese breed, introduced into Europe in the second half of the nineteenth century

Personality: a proud, beautiful dog, loyal and honest; they need frequent brushing

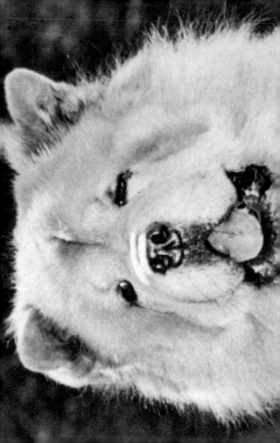

Dalmatian

Description: a strong, muscular dog of excellent proportions, fleet of foot and with a great deal of endurance

Head: longish head with a moderate stop; nose black or liver, depending on colour of coat spots

Eyes: round; black or brown

Ears: soft and carried against the head

Tail: strong at the base, tapering to a point; carried slightly curved

Body: lithe body; strong neck; straight front legs

Coat: short, hard and dense, glossy to the eye

Colour: a pure white ground colour, with clearly-defined spots of either black or liver-brown; spots on the body should be larger than those elsewhere

Sizes: dogs' height 55.9-61cm (22-24in), bitches' height 50.8-58.4cm (20-23in); weight 25kg (55lb)

Origin: thought to have originated in Yugoslavia, the breed was developed in Britain to today's high standard

Personality: playful, with a good temperament; independent, but needs a lot of human attention

French bulldog

Description: a courageous, active small bull-dog, with distinctive bat ears

Head: the skull should be flat between the ears, with a domed forehead, a short pug nose and loose black lips; a pronounced stop; a powerful muzzle

Eyes: dark, round and slightly protruding

Ears: bat-like, being broad at the base, rounded at the tips and carried erect

Tail: short; thick at the root

Body: barrel-chested, with round ribs; no dewlap

Coat: fine-textured; short; smooth and glossy

Colour: brindle, pied or fawn

Sizes: height 30.5cm (12in); dogs' weight 12.7kg (28lb), bitches' weight 10.9kg (24lb)

Origin: a native of France, with some English bulldog blood

Personality: an affectionate, companionable dog; sensitive, and a good guard dog for the apartment

Poodle (standard)

Description: active, elegant dogs that hold themselves proudly

Head: a rectilinear head and in proportion to its body; flat cheeks; black nose, except for brown and *café-au-lait* coloured dogs; their noses are liver

Eyes: black or brown

Ears: hanging along the cheeks

Tail: set high; docked to less than half-length

Body: solid neck, slightly arched

Coat: curly or corded and clipped

Colour: all single solid colours acceptable

Sizes: measured to the highest point of the shoulder, the height must be above 38.1cm (15in)

Origin: descended from the barbet, a French water dog; exactly where the poodle was developed is arguable, but possibly France, Germany, Denmark or Russia

Personality: good-natured and intelligent.

The miniature poodle is the same in every respect as the standard poodle, except for size; the height of the miniature poodle should be between 27.9-38.1cm (11-15in).

Schnauzer (standard)

Description: a robust dog, of medium size, squarely built

Head: elongated, with strong muzzle and well-developed black nose and an accentuated stop

Eyes: dark and oval

Ears: all schnauzers in Germany have their ears cropped, which is not permissible in the UK

Tail: docked to about two-thirds of its length

Body: should not be dwarflike; the neck should be long and elegant, the front legs straight

Coat: hard, coarse hair; a long, bristly beard; wavy hair is not acceptable

Colour: black or salt-and-pepper

Sizes: dogs' height 49.5cm (19.5in), bitches' height 45.7cm (18in); weight 15kg (33lb)

Origin: descended from ancient terriers and bred in Bavaria for many years, being first exhibited there in 1879 as wire-haired Pinschers

Personality: lively, bold dog which is also affectionate and devoted; the schnauzer is regarded as being a long-lived dog

Shih Tzû

Description: an arrogant, lively dog, classified in the USA as a toy, the Shih Tzû is a typical drawing-room dog

Head: a round head, wide between the eyes; a square muzzle; black nose; thick beard and moustache

Eyes: dark, large and round

Ears: long and pendent, they are lost in the dog's hair

Tail: thick and rolled over the dog's back

Body: small, finely-boned

Coat: double-coated, with an abundance of long and dense hair, which should not be curly

Colour: all colours acceptable, with a white blaze on the forehead and a white tip to the tail, which are considered assets

Sizes: height 26.7cmm (10.5in) maximum; weight 4.5-6.4kg (10-14lb)

Origin: originating in Tibet, the Shih Tzû was presented to the Chinese court in the seventeenth century, arriving in Europe about 50 years ago

Personality: alert, brave and hardy, the dog is also long-lived

Afghan hound

Description: a large, extraordinarily beautiful and aristocratic dog, with a dignified appearance and a silky rich coat

Head: long, straight and narrow; a slightly convex skull; powerful jaws; nose is black or liver

Eyes: dark or golden and of triangular shape

Ears: carried flat against the head and well covered in long silky hair

Tail: loops into a circle

Body: statuesque stance, with long straight front legs and long powerful neck

Coat: dense, silky, long hair; short along the back, and a tuft on the top of the head

Colour: all colours acceptable

Sizes: dogs' height 68.6-73.6cm (27-29in); bitches' height 61-68.6cm (24-27in); weight 26.4-29.1kg (58-64lb)

Origin: an ancient breed, with its origins somewhere in the Middle East, but not established in Europe until the early twentieth century

Personality: sweet, sensitive and very popular; they need careful training, which they respond to with love and loyalty

Basenji

Description: a lightly-built, finely-boned dog, with a wrinkled, loose-fitting skin

Head: pronounced wrinkles on the forehead; flat skull; pointed muzzle and black or slightly rose-tinted nose

Eyes: brown, almond-shaped

Ears: pricked and turned open to the front

Tail: tightly curled over its back

Body: neck well arched; muscular body and thighs covered in a slack skin; a gait with front legs carried straight forward, like a horse's

Coat: short and glossy

Colour: rich chestnut or black, with white markings or tricolour

Sizes: dogs' height 43.2cm (17in), bitches' height 40.6cm (16in); dogs' weight 10.9kg (24lb), bitches' weight 10kg (22lb)

Origin: an ancient breed, from central Africa, only establishing itself in Europe in the middle of the twentieth century

Personality: the Basenji does not bark, but makes a soft cry. A very clean dog, cheerful and good with children

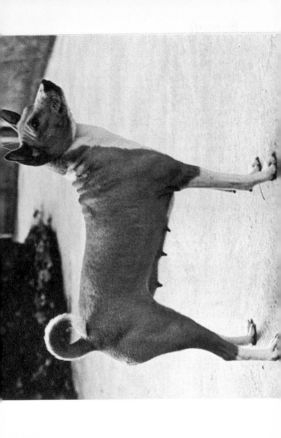

Basset hound

Description: a compact, short-legged hound with heavy bone structure

Head: large, well-proportioned, with a dome-shaped skull; the skin on the head is loose-fitting, forming folds; the nose is black

Eyes: dark

Ears: hang down like pendulums and big enough to reach beyond the tip of the nose if pulled forward

Tail: slightly curved, carried gaily

Body: prominent breastbone, but not a deep chest; powerful neck and pronounced dewlap

Coat: short, smooth but not too fine

Colour: all hound colours are acceptable

Sizes: height 33-38.1cm (13-15in); weight 18.2-22.7kg (40-50lb)

Origin: first shown in Paris in 1863, it was recognised in Britain as early as 1883, and by the American Kennel Club in 1964

Personality: mild, friendly and affectionate; a good-natured companion dog; sometimes inclined to being slow and stubborn

Beagle

Description: small, active hounds of great character, developed to hunt the hare

Head: dome-shaped skull; pointed muzzle with distinct stop; black nose, with open nostrils

Eyes: dark brown

Ears: long, wide, hanging against the cheeks

Tail: medium length, carried rather high

Body: well-sprung ribs, extending well back; powerful loins; longish neck with slight dewlap; strong, round feet

Coat: smooth, short

Colour: all hound colours acceptable

Sizes: height 33-40.6cm (13-16in); weight 8.2-13.6kg (18-30lb)

Origin: one of the oldest purebred British hounds, popular with monarchs for hunting

Personality: clean and quiet, these cheerful and affectionate hounds are now extremely popular as companion dogs

Bloodhound

Description: a tracker of great renown, big and powerful but somewhat slow

Head: large, with loose wrinkled skin over cheeks and forehead; black nose, pendent lips

Eyes: dark hazel-brown

Ears: long, hanging and low-set

Tail: curled high over the back

Body: strongly-built, standing over a good area of ground with a very free gait

Coat: short, hard hair

Colour: black and tan; liver and tan, or red

Sizes: dogs' height 63.5-68.6cm (25-27in), bitches' height 58.4-63.5cm(23-25in); weight 18.2-21.8kg (40-48lb)

Origin: a purebred hound, direct descendent of the Celtic hound

Personality: timid, good-natured and easily lovable hound, with a magnificent sense of smell; quiet by nature, this is not a good guard dog

Borzoi

Description: a large, handsome dog; very elegant and a fast, ferocious hunter

Head: long, thin and narrow, with a slightly arched muzzle and black nose

Eyes: dark, oblong

Ears: laid back on the neck

Tail: long and carried low

Body: short, slightly arched back; narrow chest

Coat: long, silky, wavy or curly but not woolly and a heavy mane at the neck

Colour: white; gold in various shades; tan shaded with black; unicolour or white with markings

Sizes: dogs' height over 73.6cm (29in), bitches' height over 68.6cm (27in); weight 34.1-45.5kg (75-100lb)

Origin: originating in Arabia, the Borzoi was introduced into Russia and developed there from the beginning of the seventeenth century, finally arriving in Britain towards the end of the nineteenth century

Personality: docile and quiet, a good-looking loyal companion; needs plenty of exercise and is apt to be stubborn

Dachshund (long-haired)

Description: long-bodied, short-legged, vigorous dog with a knowing expression

Head: long and tapering, with the forehead slightly arched and extending to the bridge of the nose without stop

Eyes: oval; dark red or brown/black

Ears: hang along the cheeks

Tail: carried in line with the back; well covered with long hair, which forms a flag

Body: strongly protruding sternum and retracted abdomen

Coat: long, soft and glossy; can be either straight or with some waviness; there are also short-haired (smooth) and wire-haired varieties

Colour: black and tan; dark brown with tan shadings; dark red; red; brindle, dapple or tiger-marked

Sizes: height 12.7-22-9cm (5-9in); dogs' weight up to 8.2kg (18lb), bitches' weight 7.7kg (17lb); there are heavier-weight dachshunds, in a range extending from these standards upwards

Origin: originating from the ancient Teckel and developed in Germany, the long-haired dachshund was the result of crossing long-coated spaniels with short-haired dachshunds

Personality: intelligent, spirited dogs, with a cheerful and affectionate nature

Dachshund (miniature short-haired)

Description: in all respects, except for size, the miniature smooth or short-haired dachshund should be similar to the standard smooth-haired

Head: elongated, with a slightly convex skull; long muzzle; black nose; dachshunds usually have 42 strong teeth and an equally strong jaw

Eyes: dark red or brown/black

Ears: mobile, hanging along the cheeks

Tail: carried in line with the back

Body: long-bodied, short-legged, with head held boldly; the long back is both broad and muscular

Coat: short, dense and smooth; free of curl

Colour: all colours acceptable, with the exception of white

Sizes: weight should be about 4.5kg (10lb) but not exceeding 5kg (11lb)

Origin: a very old-established German breed, the result of crossings including the dwarf hound and the earth dog, with the German standard for the breed having been set in 1879

Personality: developed from their role as den-hunting dogs, the dachshunds are courageous and tenacious; they are proud and good barkers, with a cheerful nature

Finnish Spitz

Description: a beautifully-defined hunting dog, sturdy and good-looking with a proud carriage

Head: the muzzle is pointed, the stop clearly defined

Eyes: dark

Ears: erect; triangular; set high on the head

Tail: curved over its back, to the side

Body: short, muscular neck; deep chest and a retracted abdomen

Coat: double-coated, with a light undercoat and short smooth outer coat

Colour: brownish-red or yellowish-red; white markings to chest, feet and under tail are acceptable

Sizes: dogs' height 43.2-50.8ccm (17-20in), bitches' height 39.3-45.7cm (15.5-18in); weight 11.4-13.6kg (25-30lb)

Origin: the national breed of Finland, where it was bred for hunting and as a watchdog on farms; its standard was set at the beginning of the nineteenth century and although introduced into Britain in 1927, it is still not recognised in America

Personality: loyal and courageous, their friendliness is deceptive as they are first-rate guard dogs

Greyhound

Description: robust and vigourous, the greyhound is most graceful when running at full speed

Head: long head with chiselled muzzle; the skull wide between the ears, and a black pointed nose

Eyes: dark

Ears: small, thin rose-shaped

Tail: slightly curved and carried low

Body: long, well-muscled neck; front legs long and straight; broad back; muscular slightly arched loin; broad muscular thighs

Coat: short and fine, tight to the body

Colour: black; white; red; fawn; fallow; brindle; multi-coloured or colour and white markings

Sizes: dogs' height 71.1-78.7 (28-31in), bitches' height 68.6-71.1cm (27-28in); weight 27.3-31.8kg (60-70lb)

Origin: an ancient breed, possibly descended from an Arab greyhound; developed in Britain, it is now the epitome of the hunting and racing dog

Personality: sensitive and intelligent, but not suited to apartment life as they need long daily exercising

Irish wolfhound

Description: the largest of breeds, the Irish wolfhound is an imposing and powerful animal
Head: long head with slightly pointed muzzle
Eyes: big and dark
Ears: low, hanging folded back to the neck
Tail: slightly curved
Body: body is arched and very muscular; strong shoulders; a deep chest and retracted abdomen; long back and well-arched loins
Coat: rough and hardy, long over the eyes and under the jaw
Colour: grey; brindle; red; black, fawn or white
Sizes: dogs' height 78.7cm (31in) minimum, bitches' height 71.1cm (28in) minimum; dogs' weight 54.4kg (120lb) minimum, bitches' weight 40.9kg (90lb) minimum

Origin: carefully bred by the Irish for hunting wolves, it nearly disappeared along with the wolves, but was successfully rescued at the end of the nineteenth century

Personality: patient, thoughtful and generous; excellent companions if you have the space and are able to give them the freedom to run

Otterhound

Description: a stocky, good-sized shaggy-coated hound, very much at home in the water with its webbed feet

Head: long, with convex skull, black nose and thick lips

Eyes: deep and dark

Ears: long and hanging

Tail: carried high, with a sabre-like curve

Body: muscular neck with prominent dewlap

Coat: double-coated, with a water-resistant undercoat of short woolly hair and an outer coat of strong, hard and bristly hair which is 7.6-15.2cm (3-6in) long on the back

Colour: any colour or colour combination is acceptable

Sizes: height 61-68.6cm (24-27in); weight 30-35kg (66-77lb)

Origin: an old-established breed, emerging at the beginning of the nineteenth century as the product of crossings involving rough-haired terriers, Welsh harriers and the bloodhound, among others

Personality: a friendly, affectionate and boisterous dog; very inquisitive; fast and untiring in the water; the otterhound can be a good friend

Pharoah hound

Description: a graceful, strong and very fast dog; a passionate rabbit-hunter, hunting by scent

Head: a long, flat skull; a slight stop and a strong jaw; a tan nose, speckled with pink

Eyes: small, can be either brown or amber

Ears: large and held erect

Tail: carried low, with a slight curve

Body: long back with a slight slope; narrow chest and the abdomen is retracted; a thin, muscular neck

Coat: short and shiny; free of feathering

Colour: tan with indiscriminate white markings, or solid bright tan

Sizes: dogs' height 55.9-71.1cm (22-28in), bitches' height 53.3-66cm (21-26in)

Origin: an ancient Egyptian dog, depicted on temple walls; the breed was established in Spain by the Saracens

Personality: a very playful, friendly dog; intelligent and loyal; a pleasant companion, but one which needs frequent long runs

Rhodesian ridgeback

Description: the dog does have a ridge running along the length of the back, which is formed by hair growing in the opposite direction to the rest of the coat

Head: elongated, with a very strong muzzle and jaws; black or brown nose, depending on coat colour; a flat skull, with a definite stop

Eyes: round and dark

Ears: wide, hanging close to the head

Tail: slightly curved towards the end

Body: powerful limbs and sturdy, heavy-set body with a thick muscular neck

Coat: short, dense coat which is smooth and glossy

Colour: wheaten or reddish fawn; white markings on the chest are acceptable, and also to the toes

Sizes: dogs' height 63.5-68.6cm (25-27in), bitches' height 61-66cm (24-26in); dogs' weight 34.1-36.4kg (75-80lb), bitches' weight 29.6-31.8kg (65-70lb)

Origin: a native of South Africa, having been developed by the Boers towards the end of the nineteenth century

Personality: a good, obedient dog and very hardy; the ridgeback can be extremely ferocious in the hunt, where it is deployed against big game

Saluki

Description: an elegant, graceful dog, very well-proportioned and with a dignified expression

Head: long, thin and narrow, with a slightly arched muzzle and black nose

Eyes: large, may be either light or dark brown

Ears: long, carried back on its neck and covered in long silky hair

Tail: set low and carried naturally in a curve and well feathered on the underside

Body: long, slender neck with muscular shoulders; elongated body

Coat: long and wavy, smooth with a soft silky texture

Colour: white; cream; fawn; golden; tan with black; tricolour; variations of these colours are also acceptable

Sizes: height 58.4-71.1cm (23-28in); weight 13.2-30kg (29-66lb)

Origin: possibly the oldest domesticated dog, the result of crossings between Egyptian and Asiatic greyhounds

Personality: a lithe, agile dog; being affectionate and friendly to children, the saluki has exceptional hearing and is therefore a useful watchdog

Whippet

Description: they represent a careful balance between the power of speed and grace
Head: flat on top; long and lean, tapering to the muzzle, and with a powerful jaw
Eyes: pronounced, lively and dark
Ears: small and rose-shaped
Tail: pointed, held down between the legs
Body: deep chest with long broad back, an elongated arched neck and retracted abdomen
Coat: fine, short and close
Colour: any solid colour or mixture of colours is acceptable
Sizes: dogs' height 48.3cm (19in), bitches' height 44.5cm (17.5in); dogs' weight 8.2-12.7kg (18-28lb), bitches' weight 5.5-9.1kg (12-20lb)

Origin: developed in Britain at the end of the nineteenth century, the whippet was the result of many crossings which included the greyhound, the Italian greyhound and the terrier

Personality: carefree and affectionate, the whippet is a docile character; resistant to illness and long-lived

Glossary

Apple head: a skull that is domed or rounded; usually a fault, except where stated as being a virtue of the breed standard

Beard: long, bushy whiskers on the chin

Bitch: female dog

Bone: a dog is said to be well-boned when its limbs both look and feel strong, without being heavy or coarse

Breed: a breed is a group of similar dogs, the looks and physical appearances of which are continued from one generation to the next without change. Most of today's breeds have resulted from artificial selection by people, rather than from natural selection.

Brindle: colouration arrived at when light and dark hairs appear in the coat, usually involving grey, tawny or brown backgrounds

Brush: a bushy, fox-like tail

Cat feet: round feet, short and compact; not splayed; for example, those of terriers

Coat: the hair that covers the dog's body. It can be very short; short; long; hard; soft; straight; wiry; wavy; woolly; silky; sleek or curly in length and texture, and in colour unicoloured (single colour coat); bicoloured (when comprised of two colours) and tricolour (three colours); the coat may also be shaded

Cobby: a compact, well-muscled body, short back, well ribbed and sprung

Coupling: the length of the dog's body measured between the last rib and the pelvis

Cropped: unacceptable in Britain and some American states, but accepted elsewhere for some breeds for which the ears are cut (cropped) to erect shapes

Dentition: the dog's teeth are fully developed before it is one year old, and the bite described is either scissors or pincers

Dew-claw: a claw growing on the inside of the leg, usually removed but often retained in mountain dog breeds

Dewlap: skin that hangs in a fold at the base of the dog's throat

Docked: carried out to the dogs when quite young; the tail is cut (docked) either short or to a prescribed length

Ears: like the coat, the ears are an important feature of the breed's standard, and may be long or short; small; large; natural or docked; bat-like; folded; pendent; erect, semi-erect or rose-shaped. They may be set high or low on the head, and close or wide apart.

Eyes: according to breed standards, the shape of the dog's eyes and their colours may also differ

Featherings: long, fine hair that forms a fringe, mostly to the legs (as in setters), but also on tails and ears

Flag: the feathering under the tail (as in setters), which should be longer at the base and shorter at the tip of the tail

Flecked: a shading of the coat when it is lightly ticked with other colours

Frill: long feathering around the neck (as in collies); the hair should be shorter at the throat

Fringe: see **featherings**

Gait: the way in which a dog walks or runs, being part of the dog's characteristics, and more important for hunting breeds

Gay: refers to a tail when carried curled up over the back or, in the case of some hounds, erect

Gestation: the gestation period is the time it takes for the embryo to develop in the mother's body; average 60-65 days for dogs; the time varies depending on a number of factors, including breed, the mother's age, and the number of puppies in the litter

Grooming: the cutting of a dog's coat, usually to breed standards

Hare-feet: the digits of the feet are well-separated and long

Heat: the time of fertility in the bitch; normally lasts for about three weeks, twice a year, and starts when she is about nine months old

Hocks: joint on the outer side of the hind leg below the stifle, corresponding to the human heel

Hound-marked: patches on the body conforming to the pattern of hound markings; applied to fox terriers

Limbs: the front and rear legs perform different functions, the front being used mainly for support and the more muscular rear legs for pro-pulsion

Mask: the colour difference of the muzzle or fore-face to the coat colour

Merle: a colour mix of blue and grey hairs which are ticked or streaked with black

Parti-coloured: a bicoloured dog, usually red and white or black and white, in which the two colours are of equal proportion

Pedigree: shown in a written document when a purebred puppy is bought and transferred to the new owner. Approved by the national canine association, it details the genealogy of the dog for several past generations

Pied: when the two colours in a bicoloured dog appear in irregular patches and in one colour more than the other

Pigmentation: the chemical colouration that is natural in the animal's tissues

Plumb: it is necessary, according to some breed standards, for the front legs to be perfectly vertical (plumb)

Plumes: soft, long hairs on the tail. Like a brush tail, where the hairs are usually coarse

Pregnancy: see **gestation**

Prick-eared: when the ears are carried erect, as in the Chow Chow

Pug: when the muzzle is flattened

Puppy: a dog under one year old

Over-shot: when the upper teeth overshoot the lower teeth; this is generally unacceptable

Roached: the convex arching of a dog's back, as in the Dandie Dinmont

Roan: white hair on the dog's coat is thickly mixed with black, reddish or blue hairs

Rose-eared: the ear folds or twists over, revealing the inside

Ruff: see **frill**

Saddle: black markings, rectangular in shape, found on the back and upper flanks

Self-marked: a unicoloured dog, with white or pale markings to the chest, the feet and the tail, either on its tip or underneath

Speckles: very small markings of dark or black on a white or light-coloured coat

Splay-feet: when the toes are wide-set, usually in sporting breeds

Standard: the actual specification of acceptable norms laid down by the breed club as a guide to the ideal physical characteristics of that breed. There is a set standard for each recognised breed which details height, weight, coat (hair), coat (colour), eye colour, skeletal details, carriage, tail (length), skull shape, muzzle, ears and legs. In addition, it describes the character of the breed and a list of unacceptable points.

Stifle: the joint on the inner side of the rear legs, which functions like the human knee joint

Stop: the term used to describe the depression in the head which falls in front of and between the eyes, the step down from the skull to the muzzle; corresponding to the bridge on the nose, the stop is an important feature of most breeds.

Stripping: the grooming of various breeds which involves the thinning of the coat by pulling out the excess hair with the fingers; carried out by an expert at the right time of the year, this operation is completely painless.

Tail: important in size, shape and carriage; the tail may be docked, short or long, thick or thin and carried high, low, curved over the back, up and to the side. It may be a plumed, sabre, otter, squirrel, ring, sickle, screw or gay tail.

Topknot: the longer hair at the top of the head, usually very fine and often needing to be tied up

Toy: the smallest size of a breed that also appears in set standards for the larger sizes

Tricolour: see **coat**

Trout marks: small reddish markings on a light background, the marks being reminiscent of those on trout fish

Undercoat: in double-coated dogs, the undercoat gives protection against cold and wet, and is usually soft and woolly textured

Undershot: when the lower jaw and teeth project beyond the upper.

Whiskers: the neat, tidy beard of terriers, which is not as dense as a full beard

Withers: the point of the first dorsal vertebra on a dog's back, from which the height of the dog is measured

Wrinkle: loose folds of skin on the face and brows, for example on bloodhounds

Index

Afghan hound 152
Airedale terrier 70
Australian terrier 72
Basenji 154
Basset hound 156
Beagle 158
Belgian sheepdog (Groenendael) 38
Bloodhound 160
Border collie 40
Border terrier 74
Borzoi 162
Boston terrier 136
Boxer 42
Bull mastiff 44
Bull terrier 76
Bulldog 138
Cairn terrier 78
Cavalier King Charles spaniel 106
Chihuahua 108
Chow Chow 140
Cocker spaniel 24
Dachshund (long-haired) 164
Dachshund (miniature short-haired) ... 166
Dalmatian 142
Dandie Dinmont 80
Dobermann Pinscher 48
English cocker spaniel 26
English setter 18
English springer spaniel 28

English Toy terrier (Black and Tan)	118
Field spaniel	30
Finnish Spitz	168
Fox terrier (wire-haired)	82
French bulldog	144
German shepherd dog (Alsatian)	50
German short-haired pointer	12
Golden retriever	14
Gordon setter	20
Great Dane	52
Greyhound	170
Griffon Bruxellois	112
Irish setter	22
Irish terrier	84
Irish water spaniel	32
Irish wolfhound	172
Italian greyhound	114
Jack Russell terrier	86
Japanese Chin	116
King Charles spaniel	118
Labrador retriever	16
Lakeland terrier	88
Löwchen	120
Maltese	122
Mastiff	54
Norfolk terrier	90
Norwich terrier	92
Old English sheepdog	56
Otterhound	174

Papillon	124
Pekingese	126
Pharoah hound	176
Pointer	10
Pomeranian	128
Poodle (standard)	146
Poodle (toy)	130
Pug	132
Pyrenean mountain dog	58
Rhodesian ridgeback	178
Rottweiler	60
Rough collie	46
Saluki	180
Samoyed	64
Schnauzer (standard)	148
Scottish terrier	94
Sealyham terrier	96
Shih Tzû	150
Siberian husky	66
Skye terrier	98
St Bernard	62
Staffordshire bull terrier	100
Sussex spaniel	34
Welsh corgi	68
Welsh springer spaniel	36
Welsh terrier	102
West Highland White terrier	104
Whippet	182
Yorkshire terrier	134